big
NATE
PAYBACK TIME!

Complete Your *Big Nate* Collection

SPECIAL COLLECTIONS

big NATE
PAYBACK TIME!

by LINCOLN PEIRCE

Andrews McMeel
PUBLISHING®

PRINCIPAL NICHOLS, I'VE RECENTLY DEVELOPED A **SEVERE** ALLERGY TO MRS. GODFREY!

IF I COME WITHIN TEN FEET OF THE WOMAN, I START SNEEZING UNCONTROLLABLY!

CLEARLY, YOUR COURSE OF ACTION IS **CRYSTAL CLEAR!**

TO ONE OF US, ANYWAY.

A KID'S ALLERGIC TO PEANUTS, YOU MAKE THE SCHOOL PEANUT-FREE, RIGHT?

The second half was closely contested, and it was only the heroics of goalkeeper *Nate Wright* that enabled the Bobcats to maintain their lead.

Nate made several saves that can only be described as superhuman. Each time the Hawks threatened to knot the score, he turned them away in spine-tingling fashion.

When the final horn sounded, Nate's teammates rushed to him in elation. Some hoisted him on their shoulders. Others simply gazed at him in awe.

As the sun set, Nate lingered on the field, seemingly reluctant to abandon the goal he had so magnificently protected. Then, finally, he walked slowly to the sideline.

There, he was met by a crowd of babe-a-licious cheerleaders.

"Hello, ladies," said the dark-haired dynamo to his adoring fans.

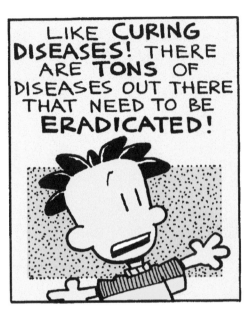

MRS. GODFREY, CAN'T I WRITE ABOUT A DIFFERENT PRESIDENT INSTEAD OF JOHN TYLER?

I'VE READ EVERYTHING ABOUT THE GUY, AND HE'S JUST NOT ALL THAT INTERESTING!

THEN IT'S YOUR JOB AS A WRITER TO **MAKE** HIM INTERESTING!

!

JOHN TYLER vs. THE ANDROIDS OF PLANET OBLIVIA

Welcome to "**FEELINGS**" with Doctor WARREN FUZZY

Today I'm talking to **PERCY PUMPKIN** about the **ANXIETY** he's been experiencing lately!

Hi, Doc.

Tell me everything, Percy.

Well, ever since I was taken out of my patch, I've had a looming sense of **DREAD**.

I keep having nightmares about being **ATTACKED**! With a **KNIFE**!

That's very disturbing.

I just **KNOW** something bad is going to happen!

There, there, Percy. Nightmares are expressions of subconscious fears... but they're **NOT REAL**! You **WON'T** be attacked with a knife! **TRUST** me!

Try to focus on **REALITY**! And think **POSITIVELY**! We'll discuss your progress at our next session!

ONE WEEK LATER...

Oh, dear.

Told ya.

LOOK AT ALL THAT **CANDY!** HOW MANY HOUSES HAVE YOU GONE TO, CHAD?

I'VE DONE ELM STREET AND PHILBY STREET SO FAR.

THOSE ARE THE SAME STREETS **WE'VE** DONE! AND YOU'VE GOT **THREE TIMES** AS MUCH CANDY AS WE DO!

IT'S THE CUTENESS FACTOR.

CHAD'S SO CUTE AND LOVABLE, ADULTS CAN'T **RESIST** HIM! THEY'LL DO ANYTHING FOR HIM! **ANYTHING!**

DUDE. HOW DOES IT FEEL TO BE AN UNSTOPPABLE TSUNAMI OF ADORABLENESS?

ME? HA HA! WHO WANTS GOOBERS?

HI, MR. STEWART! WANT YOUR LEAVES RAKED?

NO, THANK YOU. I RAKE MY OWN LEAVES.

WOW, YOU DO THIS HUGE YARD YOUR**SELF**? THAT MUST TAKE A LONG TIME.

A FEW DAYS.

AND WHAT DOES **MRS.** STEWART DO DURING THOSE "FEW DAYS"?

OH, INDOOR STUFF, I SUPPOSE.

AH-**HA!** INDOOR STUFF LIKE SPENDING HOURS AND HOURS ON THE **COMPUTER!**...

...WHERE SHE'LL JUST **HAPPEN** TO WANDER INTO A **CHAT ROOM** FOR PEOPLE TRYING TO RE-KINDLE OLD **FLAMES!**

BEFORE YOU KNOW IT, SHE'LL BE TAKING OFF FOR **MEXICO** WITH SOME HIGH SCHOOL BOY-FRIEND SHE HASN'T SEEN IN **60 YEARS!**

...ALL BECAUSE **YOU** INSISTED ON RAKING YOUR OWN LEAVES!

SLAM!

SAD HOW SOME PEOPLE JUST CAN'T HANDLE THE TRUTH.

AT THE NEXT HOUSE, I'LL DO THE TALKING.

YOU KNOW WHY MOST OF THE STAFF QUIT, GINA? BECAUSE **YOU'RE** SUCH A LOUSY EDITOR!

WHAT?

YOU NEVER LET US WRITE ABOUT ANYTHING **INTERESTING!**

JUST LAST WEEK, YOU REJECTED MY EXCLUSIVE STORY ON THE CRISIS IN THE PHYS. ED. DEPARTMENT!

"COACH JOHN'S JOCK ITCH WORSENS" DIDN'T STRIKE ME AS PARTICULARLY NEWSWORTHY.

BUT WHAT A HEADLINE!

PEOPLE DON'T WANT **NEWS** IN THEIR NEWSPAPERS, GINA! THEY WANT TO BE **ENTERTAINED!**

IF FRANCIS HERE WINS A MEDAL AT THE MATH MEET, NOBODY CARES! THAT'S NEWS!

BUT IF SOMEBODY EXPERIENCES SOME FORM OF PUBLIC HUMILIATION, THAT'S ENTERTAINMENT!

LIKE SO!

YIP!

NOW I GET IT!

MRS. GODFREY, WHAT'S THAT?

IT'S TIME FOR OUR CLASSROOM TO HAVE A **MASCOT!**

IS IT A MOUSE?

CLOSE! HE'S A GERBIL!

POOR LITTLE GUY. COOPED UP IN A GLASS CAGE INSTEAD OF RUNNING FREE IN HIS NATURAL HABITAT.

WHAT **IS** A GERBIL'S NATURAL HABITAT?

I DON'T HAVE THE FOGGIEST IDEA.

ISN'T IT THE SMALL ANIMALS AISLE AT PETSMART?

NATE, YOU CAN'T DO A BOOK REPORT ABOUT "BIPPITY BUNNY AND THE BIG BULLY"!

WHY NOT?

BECAUSE IT'S FOR **FIRST GRADERS**! SURELY YOU'VE READ SOME **OTHER** BOOKS RECENTLY!

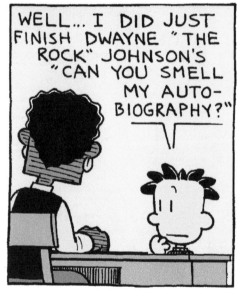

WELL... I DID JUST FINISH DWAYNE "THE ROCK" JOHNSON'S "CAN YOU SMELL MY AUTO-BIOGRAPHY?"

THAT'S NON-FICTION, NATE.

NO, NO. TURNS OUT THE WHOLE W.W.E. THING IS TOTALLY FAKE.

MS. CLARKE, "BIPPITY BUNNY AND THE BIG BULLY" MIGHT BE A KIDDIE BOOK, BUT IT'S A **GREAT STORY!**

IT'S GOT A BEGINNING, A MIDDLE, AND AN END, A PROTAGONIST AND AN ANTAGONIST, CONFLICT AND RESOLUTION! ALL THE STUFF **YOU** TOLD US ADDS UP TO A GOOD STORY!

PLUS, WHEN YOU GAVE US THE ASSIGNMENT, YOU DIDN'T SAY WE **COULDN'T** CHOOSE A KIDDIE BOOK, NOW **DID** YOU?

SO. READ IT AND WEEP.

I'M PRETTY SURE I WILL.

Peirce

In "Bippity Bunny And The Big Bully," the main character is a bunny who's just minding his own business on the school playground when, all of the sudden, along comes a bully.

Before I go any further, I should mention that all the characters in this book are animals, which gets a little annoying because there are all these species hanging out together who would NEVER hang out in real life. Like, in the background of one of the pictures, a kangaroo is playing hopscotch with a lion. Uh, I don't think so. The lion would be using the kangaroo as dental floss in about two seconds.

Anyway, this bully comes along, and I have no idea what kind of animal he's supposed to be. He doesn't have a name to tip us off, like Gary Gopher or Monty Muskrat. Everybody just calls him Todd.

Let's just say he's a woodchuck and move on.

THIS JOB IS STARTING TO GET TO ME.

YOU'VE TAUGHT HERE A LONG TIME, RIGHT, MR. GALVIN?

FORTY-TWO YEARS.

FORTY-TWO YEARS! THAT MEANS YOU TAUGHT MY DAD!

I SUPPOSE I MUST HAVE.

WHAT WAS HE LIKE BACK THEN?

WHAT WAS HIS NAME AGAIN?

MARTIN WRIGHT!

MARTIN WRIGHT... HMMM... MARTIN WRIGHT...

NNNNO... I'M DRAWING A BLANK, I'M AFRAID.

DESCRIBE WHAT HE'S LIKE NOW, AND PERHAPS I'LL REMEMBER WHAT HE WAS LIKE THEN.

WELL, HE'S...

HE...

UMMM...

YOU MAY NOT REALIZE IT, BUT TODAY WAS ONE OF THE SADDEST DAYS OF YOUR LIFE.

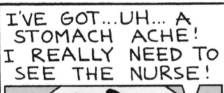

DID YOU GUYS KNOW THAT WHEN THE SCHOOL NURSE ISN'T AROUND, **COACH JOHN** FILLS IN FOR HER?

WHAT A **JOKE!** THE GUY'S A TOTAL **PSYCHO!** NURSES ARE SUPPOSED TO BE **NICE!**

WHENEVER I GO SEE THE NURSE, SHE POKES ME IN THE STOMACH AND SAYS, "HOW'S MY FAVORITE JELLY BELLY?"

I JUST HAVEN'T GROWN OUT OF MY BABY FAT YET, **OKAY?!**

POOR CHAD.

CLEAR YOUR DESKS, PEOPLE. WE'RE HAVING A POP QUIZ ON CHAPTER SIX.

GROANN...

OH, **NO**, WE'RE NOT!

IS THERE A PROBLEM, NATE?

NOT AT ALL!

JUST CALLING YOUR ATTENTION TO **THIS** LITTLE ITEM I WON BACK IN SEPTEMBER AT THE BOOSTER CLUB **RAFFLE**!

"THIS CARD ENTITLES THE HOLDER TO ONE (1) FAVOR FROM MRS. GODFREY." THAT SAYS IT ALL!

AND I'M CASHING THIS PUPPY IN! I'M ASKING MRS. GODFREY TO **CANCEL THE QUIZ!!**

YAAYY!

LOOKS LIKE YOU NEGLECTED TO READ THE **BACK** OF THAT CARD, NATE.

IT HAS AN **EXPIRATION DATE**! THAT FAVOR WAS ONLY GOOD THROUGH **OCTOBER**!

YOU HAVE FORTY MINUTES.

OH, HOW I HATE HER.

PRINCIPAL NICHOLS, I THINK THAT WE STUDENTS SHOULD HAVE A LOUNGE LIKE THE TEACHERS! A PLACE WE CAN HANG OUT!

NATE, THE SCHOOL DOESN'T HAVE ANY ROOMS TO SPARE.

SO WE'LL **CONVERT** ONE!

HOW ABOUT ROOM 212? ROOM 212 ISN'T BEING USED FOR ANYTHING IMPORTANT!

THAT'S THE SOCIAL STUDIES ROOM, NATE.

AS I SAID...

IF WE COULD ONLY FIND A ROOM THAT WASN'T BEING USED FOR ANYTHING, WE COULD TURN IT INTO SUCH AN AWESOME STUDENT LOUNGE!

I'VE GOT A BEAN BAG CHAIR I COULD DONATE!

YEAH, AND I COULD BRING IN A BOOM BOX FOR TUNES!

...AND I HAVE A CUTE POSTER OF A KITTY CLINGING TO A TREE BRANCH WITH A CAPTION THAT SAYS "HANG IN THERE"!

I'M GONNA HAVE TO VETO THAT ONE, DUDE.

WE WANT A LOUNGE, CHAD, NOT A COUNSELOR'S OFFICE.

YES?

HOWDY, MA'AM! CARE TO BUY A CALENDAR TO SUPPORT THE P.S. 38 BOOSTER CLUB?

THIS BROCHURE SHOWS THE WIDE SELECTION WE HAVE TO OFFER!

UM, I'M NOT REALLY A "CALENDAR PERSON."

BUT MAYBE SOMEONE YOU KNOW **IS**!

WITH THE HOLIDAYS COMING UP, CALENDARS MAKE GREAT **GIFTS**!

LIKE THAT FAIRY TALES ONE, FOR INSTANCE! BET YOUR GRAND-CHILDREN WOULD **LOVE** THAT ONE!

GRAND-CHILDREN?

JUST HOW OLD DO YOU THINK I **AM**?

HMM... WELL...

APPARENTLY WHEN THEY ASK THAT, THEY'RE NOT REALLY LOOKING FOR AN ANSWER.

DAD, I'M NOT ASKING FOR A DOG FOR CHRISTMAS.

YOU'RE **NOT**?

NOPE. IT WOULDN'T BE FAIR TO LEAVE A DOG AT HOME ALONE WHILE I'M AT SCHOOL!

A DOG NEEDS COMPANIONSHIP PRETTY MUCH AROUND THE CLOCK!

I AGREE!

...WHICH IS WHY I'M ASKING FOR **TWO** DOGS!

CRIPES.

I KNOW WHAT YOU'RE DOING, DAD!

YOU'RE PRETENDING YOU **DIDN'T** GET ME A DOG, SO IT'LL BE A SURPRISE WHEN YOU **DO!**

THE ONLY THING I DON'T KNOW IS **WHAT** YOU'LL GET ME! A COLLIE? A PUG? AN IRISH SETTER? A DALMATIAN?

HOW DOES A PAIR OF SNOW PANTS AND THE "BIG FAT BOOK OF SUDOKU" SOUND?

YAK YAK YAK

NATE, I'M SORRY YOU DIDN'T GET A DOG FOR CHRISTMAS, BUT YOU CAN'T LET IT AFFECT YOUR GAME!

OH YES I CAN, COACH.

I PLAY BETTER WHEN I'M MAD! INJUSTICE IS MY FUEL, AND ANGER IS MY MIGHTY ENGINE!

JUST TURN ME LOOSE AGAINST THAT OTHER TEAM, AND I'LL EAT THEIR **LUNCH!**

APPARENTLY, THE PREGAME PEP TALK I WAS PLANNING WON'T BE NECESSARY.

DID SOMEBODY MENTION LUNCH?

GREAT GAME, NATE! WOW, YOU WERE **UNSTOPPABLE!**

I WAS MOTI-VATED.

I WAS SO MAD THAT I DIDN'T GET A DOG FOR CHRISTMAS, I TURNED ALL MY FRUSTRATION INTO **DOMINATION!**

SO... YOU DIDN'T GET SOMETHING YOU WANTED, AND AS A RESULT, YOU PERFORMED EXCEPTION-ALLY WELL!

HOW **FASCINATING!**

THIS CON-VERSATION IS TAKING AN UGLY TURN.

DAD, WE'RE HAVING A BAKE SALE TO RAISE MONEY FOR THE CARTOONING CLUB.

I NEED TO BRING FOUR DOZEN PEANUT BUTTER COOKIES TO SCHOOL TOMORROW, OKAY?

I'LL BE WATCHING TV.

WHAT'S WRONG WITH THIS PICTURE?

NO IDEA. MUST BE THE CABLE.

...AND NOW LET'S ADD TWO STICKS OF BUTTER...

WHATEVER YOU SAY, CONNIE.

DAD. CUT IT OUT.

CUT WHAT OUT?

TALKING TO THE **COOKIE LADY!** SHE'S JUST A **YOUTUBE VIDEO!**

I **REALIZE** SHE'S A VIDEO, NATE, BUT I HAPPEN TO FEEL A CONNECTION WITH THIS WOMAN THAT'S **PALPABLE!**

NOTICE THAT MY BUTTER IS VERY SOFT.

I'LL SAY IT IS.

DOES "PALPABLE" MEAN "CREEPY"?

YESTERDAY MY DAD FELL IN LOVE WITH A WOMAN IN A **YOUTUBE VIDEO!**

HOW IDIOTIC IS **THAT**, BECOMING INFATUATED WITH SOMEONE YOU CAN'T HAVE, SOMEONE WHO'S COMPLETELY UNATTAINABLE, SOMEONE—

'SCUSE ME A SEC.

JENNY, M'LADY!

HM?

JENNY, DON'T YOU THINK YOU AND ARTUR SPEND AN AWFUL LOT OF TIME TOGETHER?

YES, EINSTEIN, BECAUSE HE'S MY **BOY-FRIEND**.

YEAH, YEAH, I GET IT. YOU LIKE HAVING HIM STUCK TO YOU LIKE VELCRO. FOR **NOW**.

BUT WHEN PEOPLE FOLLOW YOU AROUND ALL THE TIME, THEY END UP MAKING **PESTS** OF THEMSELVES!

YOU DON'T SAY.

OH, BELIEVE ME, I'VE SEEN IT HAPPEN.

THERE THEY GO: JENNY AND ARTUR, HOLDING HANDS AS USUAL.

NOBODY EVER HOLDS **MY** HAND LIKE THAT.

BUT HEY, THAT'S OKAY, RIGHT, SPITSY? WHO NEEDS A **GIRL** AROUND?

I'VE GOT **YOU** TO HANG OUT WITH! WE CAN HAVE PLENTY OF FUN, JUST US **GUYS**!

WURF!

THERE'S NOTHING LIKE A LITTLE MALE BONDING TO LIVEN UP AN AFTERNOON!

SNIF! SNUF!

SO! WHAT DO YOU WANT TO DO FIRST? BUILD A SNOW FORT? DIG A TUNNEL? OR...

ZOW!

?

WHY AM I STILL CHASING AFTER JENNY? WHY DO I THINK SHE'S EVER GOING TO CHANGE HER MIND ABOUT ME?

SHE DOESN'T LIKE ME! I HAVE TO ACCEPT THAT! I'VE GOT TO STOP THROWING MYSELF AT HER LIKE SOME LOVESICK PUPPY!

I'VE GOT TO HAVE ENOUGH SELF-RESPECT TO STEP ASIDE WITH **DIGNITY** AND STOP MAKING SUCH A **SPECTACLE** OF MY LIFE!

WELL, I'M GLAD TO SEE YOU'RE FINALLY—

IMPORTANT ANNOUNCEMENT, PEOPLE!

CLAP
CLAP

WHAT'S THIS I HEAR ABOUT YOU DROPPING THE TORCH YOU'VE BEEN CARRYING FOR JENNY?

IT'S TRUE! I'M DONE WAITING AROUND FOR HER!

THERE ARE **PLENTY** OF GIRLS IN THIS SCHOOL WHO'D BE **THRILLED** TO GO OUT WITH ME!

ALL I NEED TO DO IS LET THEM KNOW I'M AVAILABLE!

RIGHT. I'LL WARN THEM.

I MEAN **TELL**. I'LL **TELL** THEM.

YOU'RE NOT HELPING.

I'VE MADE A MAJOR DECISION: I'M GOING TO FORGET ABOUT JENNY AND GET ON WITH MY LIFE!

SHE'S STILL TOTALLY INFATUATED WITH ARTUR, AND I'M THROUGH WAITING FOR HER TO COME TO HER SENSES!

I DESERVE SOMEONE WHO LIKES ME FOR WHO I AM! SOMEONE I CAN BUILD SOMETHING **SPECIAL** WITH!

THAT'S WHERE **YOU** COME IN.

DO I KNOW YOU?

ROWR!

Peirce

BIANCA! I GUESS YOU'VE HEARD THAT MY CRUSH ON JENNY IS OFFICIALLY **OVER!**

YUP! I'M NEWLY ELIGIBLE, NOW THAT I'VE DECIDED JENNY'S NOT THE GIRL FOR ME!

CONSIDERING THE FACT THAT SHE'S GOING OUT WITH ARTUR, WASN'T IT **JENNY** WHO DECIDED JENNY'S NOT THE GIRL FOR YOU?

IT'S HARD TO HAVE A CONVERSATION WITH SOMEONE WHO KEEPS GOING OFF ON IRRELEVANT TANGENTS.

HELLO? YEAH, I'D LIKE TO REPORT A CRIME.

NO, NOT IN PROGRESS. EARLIER TODAY.

WHERE? AT P.S. 38. THE MIDDLE SCHOOL. UH-HUH.

OKAY, SO THE HOT LUNCH MENU SAID THAT TODAY WAS GOING TO BE PIZZA, TATER TOTS, AND PEANUT BUTTER CRISP.

THAT'S THE BEST HOT LUNCH THERE **IS**! SO OBVIOUSLY I DIDN'T BRING LUNCH FROM HOME TODAY! WHY **WOULD** I?

THEN I GOT TO THE CAFETORIUM, AND THERE WAS NO PIZZA, NO TATER TOTS, AND NO PEANUT BUTTER CRISP!

INSTEAD, THEY GAVE US **MEAT LOAF**, **3-BEAN SALAD**, AND **FRUIT COCKTAIL**!

IF THAT'S NOT A CRIME, I DON'T KNOW **WHAT IS**!!

HELLO?

HELLO?

"CRIMESTOPPERS TIP LINE"! WHAT A **JOKE**!

WOULDN'T IT BE COOL TO BE AN FBI PROFILER LIKE THESE GUYS?

UNLOCKING THE SECRETS OF THE CRIMINAL MIND TO TRACK DOWN SERIAL KILLERS AND PSYCHOS AND STUFF!

PLUS, THE JOB HAS ALL KINDS OF PERKS!

SIR, ANOTHER BODY HAS BEEN FOUND...

...AT THE PLAYBOY MANSION.

SEE?

LOVE THIS SHOW!

Peirce

DID YOU HEAR ABOUT MY PLAN, FRANCIS? I'M GOING TO BECOME AN FBI PROFILER!

I THINK TO BE A PROFILER, YOU NEED TO BE A PSYCHIATRIST.

AND TO BE A PSYCHIATRIST, YOU NEED TO GO TO MEDICAL SCHOOL.

AND TO GO TO MEDICAL SCHOOL...

MAYBE I'LL JUST BE A HUNKY FIELD AGENT WITH A TROUBLED PAST.

PRINCIPAL NICHOLS, AS A FUTURE FBI PROFILER, I HAVE SOME IMPORTANT INFORMATION TO SHARE WITH YOU!

THERE'S AN INDIVIDUAL HERE AT P.S. 38 WHO I BELIEVE IS EXTREMELY DANGEROUS!

THIS PERSON IS A SADIST, A NARCISSIST, AND A POTENTIALLY VIOLENT SOCIOPATH!

GOOD HEAVENS!

SHE'S ALSO THE WORST SOCIAL STUDIES TEACHER I'VE EVER—

THAT'S ENOUGH, SON.

TOMORROW'S GROUNDHOG DAY.

YEAH, I'VE NEVER UNDERSTOOD GROUNDHOG DAY.

I MEAN, WHO DECIDED THAT A GROUNDHOG SEEING HIS SHADOW MEANS SIX MORE WEEKS OF WINTER?

I DON'T KNOW.

WHY SIX WEEKS? WHY NOT FIVE? WHY NOT SEVEN OR EIGHT?

I DON'T KNOW.

AND IF HE **DOESN'T** SEE HIS SHADOW, THEN SPRING SUPPOSEDLY COMES EARLY! WELL, **HOW** EARLY?

I DON'T **KNOW!**

PLUS, WHY WOULD A GROUNDHOG EVEN BE **AWAKE** IN FEBRUARY? DON'T GROUNDHOGS **HIBERNATE?**

I DON'T KNOW!

WHY DIDN'T THEY PICK AN ANIMAL THAT **DOESN'T** HIBERNATE, LIKE A RACCOON?

I DON'T KNOW! I DON'T KNOW!

OR A FOX? OR A BADGER?

YAAH!

TOUCHY.

PEOPLE GET SO TENSE AROUND HOLIDAYS.

...AND NONE OF THE PENCIL SHARPENERS AROUND HERE WORK AT **ALL**!

HA HA! SO TRUE!

COMPLAIN DEPT.

HEY, NATE, CAN **I** DO A COMPLAINT?

WELL...OKAY. JUST LET ME DO ONE MORE, AND THEN YOU CAN HAVE A TURN.

THE TATER TOTS AT LUNCH YESTERDAY WERE KIND OF SOGGY.

COMPLAI DEPT.

THAT'S WHAT **I** WAS GOING TO SAY!

SORRY, CHAD. IT'S MY TABLE.

CELEBRITY CHAT!
with
DAN CUPID,
LOVE CONSULTANT

Hello, friends! As you know, Valentine's Day is an extremely busy time for yours truly!

I'm working **NON-STOP** to bring couples together!

But remember: There are many other types of affection besides **ROMANTIC** love!

There's the love of a parent for a child!... The love of a pet for its owner!...

And unfortunately, there are **SOME** types of affection that just aren't very appealing!

Observe!

SPROING!

DOINNG!

MRS. GODFREY, I MADE YOU SOME VALENTINE COOKIES!

GINA, YOU'RE **WONDERFUL!**

GAG ME.

YOU HAVE NO CHANCE WITH MOLLY BISHOP, NATE! SEVENTH-GRADE GIRLS DON'T DANCE WITH SIXTH-GRADE BOYS!

SEVENTH-GRADE GIRLS DANCE WITH **EIGHTH**-GRADE BOYS! AND **SIXTH**-GRADE GIRLS DANCE WITH **SEVENTH**-GRADE BOYS!

SO WHERE DOES THAT LEAVE THE SIXTH-GRADE BOYS?

STANDING BY THE FOOD TABLE, COMMENTING ON THE SNACKS.

THESE CHIPS ARE STALE.

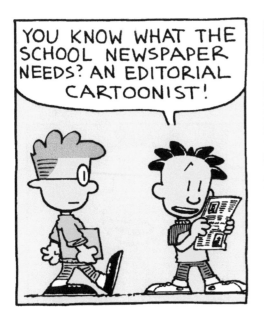

YOU KNOW WHAT THE SCHOOL NEWSPAPER NEEDS? AN EDITORIAL CARTOONIST!

EDITORIAL CARTOONISTS EXPOSE INJUSTICE AND HYPOCRISY! THEY'RE **TRUTH-TELLERS!**

WHAT TRUTH DO YOU THINK NEEDS TELLING?

THAT MRS. GODFREY IS A SATANIC PANT LOAD.

AND YOU'RE JUST THE GUY TO TELL IT.

RIGHT! IN A WACKY, CARTOONY WAY!

PRINCIPAL NICHOLS, DO YOU LIKE EDITORIAL CARTOONS?

I DO INDEED!

SO IF I WANTED TO DO AN EDITORIAL CARTOON FOR THE SCHOOL PAPER, YOU'D SUPPORT THAT?

I BELIEVE SO, YES.

AND WE AGREE THAT EDITORIAL CARTOONS OFTEN FEATURE GROTESQUE DEPICTIONS OF PEOPLE IN POWER! AWESOME!

UH... WHICH PEOPLE IN POWER?

GUYS! HE SAID YES!

Y'KNOW, RANDY WOULDN'T WANT TO KILL YOU IF YOU HADN'T DUMPED YOUR **LUNCH** ON HIM IN THE CAFETORIUM!

THAT WAS AN **ACCIDENT!**

ALL I WAS TRYING TO DO WAS SAVE AMELIA FROM TALKING TO HIM! SHE OBVIOUSLY WANTED HIM TO LEAVE HER **ALONE!**

THEN AFTER THAT, I FIGURED SHE AND I WOULD SIT DOWN TOGETHER, EAT LUNCH, AND GET TO KNOW EACH OTHER A LITTLE BETTER!

...FOLLOWED, PERHAPS, BY A FEW ROMANTIC SPARKS.

HE HAS A VERY ACTIVE FANTASY LIFE.

HEY, I JUST THOUGHT OF SOMETHING! IF I GET DETENTION, I **CAN'T** MEET RANDY ON THE SOCCER FIELD AT 3:30!

BETTER GET IN TROUBLE QUICK, THEN. SCHOOL'S OVER IN TWO MINUTES.

I'LL ONLY NEED TWO **SECONDS!**

MR. GALVIN, YOU ARE A **STIFF!** YOU'RE A STEAMING HOT PLATE FULL OF **BORING!**

TRY PINCHING HIM.

HELLO? HE**LLO!**

ZZZZZZ

SNAP SNAP

Peirce

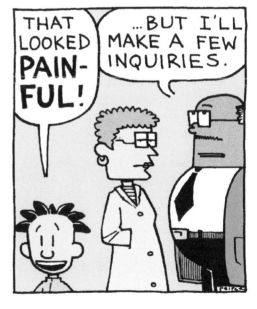

SO THAT'S THE WHOLE STORY. AM I IN TROUBLE?

NO, NATE, YOU'RE NOT IN TROUBLE.

IT SEEMS CLEAR THAT YOU WERE TRYING TO **AVOID** A FIGHT, NOT **ENGAGE** IN ONE!

BUT IF RANDY EVER THREATENS YOU AGAIN, COME TO **ME**! LET **ME** HANDLE IT!

HEY, I HANDLED IT JUST **FINE!**

NATE, A STUDENT HAS A DISLOCATED SHOULDER.

AND IT WASN'T ME. THAT'S WHAT I MEAN BY "FINE."

PETER, EeF M'BOY!

OH NO.

WHAT ARE **YOU** DOING HERE? IT ISHN'T "BOOK BUDDY" DAY!

YOU'RE RIGHT!

IT'S **WRITING** DAY! MRS. BIGBEE WANTS YOU TO WRITE A **STORY!**

YESH! FINALLY, A CHANCE TO **CREATE!**

THE FORMAT YOU'LL USE IS: ① SOMEBODY ② WANTED ③ BUT ④ SO!

WHAT? WHAT ISH **THAT?**

IT'S HOW YOU MAKE A STORY! ①**SOMEBODY** ②**WANT**-ED SOMETHING, ③**BUT** THEY COULDN'T GET IT, ④**SO** THEY DID **THIS!**

BUT THE SHTORY I WANT TO TELL ISH MORE **COMPLEX** THAN THAT! IT'SH A MULTI-GENERATIONAL **EPIC!**

SORRY. GOTTA USE THE FORMAT.

SHOMEBODY, A YOUNG GENIUSH, **WANTED** TO WRITE AN ORIGINAL SHTORY, **BUT** HISH IDIOT BOOK BUDDY WOULDN'T LET HIM!

...**SHO** THE YOUNG GENIUSH TOOK HISH **REVENGE** WHEN THE BOOK BUDDY WASHN'T EXPECTING IT! THE END!

I THINK PETER'S READY TO START WORKING INDE-PENDENTLY.

Check out these and other books from
Andrews McMeel Publishing

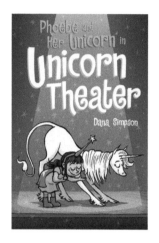

Andrews McMeel Publishing
a division of Andrews McMeel Universal
1130 Walnut Street, Kansas City, Missouri 64106

www.andrewsmcmeel.com

ISBN: 978-1-5248-5126-2

Library of Congress Control Number: 2018950018

These strips appeared in newspapers from
September 22, 2014, through March 14, 2015.

Big Nate can be viewed on the Internet at
www.gocomics.com/big_nate.

ATTENTION: SCHOOLS AND BUSINESSES
Andrews McMeel books are available at quantity discounts with bulk purchase for educational, business, or sales promotional use. For information, please e-mail the Andrews McMeel Publishing Special Sales Department:
specialsales@amuniversal.com.

CPSIA information can be obtained
at www.ICGtesting.com
Printed in the USA
LVHW071951210521
688194LV00005B/322